Louise Hay
and Kristina Tracy

I Think, I Am!

Teaching Kids the Power of Affirmations

Illustrated by
Manuela Schwarz

Carlsbad, California • New York City
London • Sydney • Johannesburg
Vancouver • Hong Kong • New Delhi

Dear Parents and Teachers,

My name is Louise Hay. I have spent my career teaching people that their thoughts create their lives. I've written many books that have helped people discover their self-worth. However, I have always believed that if children could learn the power of their thoughts early on, their journey through life would be happier and more rewarding.

This book, which I have written with my friend Kristina Tracy, gives you a way to teach your children about affirmations. Affirmations are the thoughts and words we use in our daily lives. Words of worry, anger, and fear are negative affirmations. Optimistic words of hope, happiness, and love are positive affirmations.

Inside *I Think, I Am!* you will see examples of kids turning "negative" thoughts into positive words and actions. You can practice doing this at home with your child. I like to teach children to do "mirror work," which is saying your positive affirmations in front of a mirror. A mirror is a very powerful tool because it connects you to the words you are saying. A great affirmation to start with is "I love myself." Say this, or any other positive affirmation, over and over, and notice the difference!

Love, LuLu

Copyright © 2008 by Louise Hay

Published and distributed in the United States by: Hay House, Inc.: www.hayhouse.com • **Published and distributed in Australia by:** Hay House Australia Pty. Ltd.: www.hayhouse.com.au • **Published and distributed in the United Kingdom by:** Hay House UK, Ltd.: www.hayhouse.co.uk • **Published and distributed in the Republic of South Africa by:** Hay House SA (Pty), Ltd.: www.hayhouse.co.za • **Distributed in Canada by:** Raincoast Books: www.raincoast.com • **Published in India by:** Hay House Publishers India: www.hayhouse.co.in

Design and editorial assistance: Jenny Richards • *Illustrations:* © Manuela Schwarz

Library of Congress Control Number: 2008928694

ISBN: 978-1-4019-2208-5

15 14 13 12 11 10 9 8
1st edition, October 2008

Printed in the United States of America

Certified Chain of Custody
Promoting Sustainable Forestry
www.sfiprogram.org
SFI-01268

SUSTAINABLE FORESTRY INITIATIVE

SFI label applies to the text stock

Af·fir·ma·tion

Words that you think or say, and believe to be true.

Did you know that the things you think and say have the power to make a big difference in your life? When you say something over and over, you start to believe it is true; and what you believe creates what you do and what happens to you. These kinds of thoughts and words are called affirmations. Learning to turn your unhappy (negative) thoughts into positive affirmations is a great thing to practice. Here's how it works:

POSITIVE AFFIRMATION

NEGATIVE THOUGHT

Change to:

Nobody Likes Me.

I Love Myself, and other People Love Me, too!

POSITIVE THINGS HAPPEN!

=

"Hi, want to be friends?"

The more you can learn to do this, the happier you will be. Keep reading to see more examples of kids turning negative thoughts into positive affirmations.

When waiting around is not what you planned, you may start to have negative thoughts . . .

This LiNE is so LoNg. We wiLL NeveR get iN to the faiR.

Picture the fun you will have and say . . .

I MAKE TODAY GREAT!

Have you ever wished you looked
different or more like someone else?
You might feel like saying . . .

I don't Like
My haiR. I wish it
weRe Like heRs!

Instead, look in the mirror every day and repeat...

I LOVE MYSELF JUST THE WAY I AM.

If your friends all want you to go their way, it's easy to think . . .

If I don't do what they want, they will be mad at me.

Do what is right for you and tell yourself . . .

I STAND UP FOR WHAT IS IMPORTANT TO ME.

When you don't want to pay
attention, you may believe . . .

This isn't about
me, so I don't
need to listen.

Remember that life has a lot to teach you, and think . . .

I LOVE TO LEARN NEW THINGS.

When you are feeling all alone,
unhappy thoughts might creep in . . .

Why don't they want to talk to me?

Help these feelings go away by telling yourself . . .

I AM SURROUNDED BY LOVE.

If it seems easier to sit back and
watch than to help, you may think . . .

I wish someone
would help him get
on that pony!

Change your thoughts and say . . .

I HAPPILY HELP WHEREVER I CAN.

Even though you have many great things in your life, sometimes you'll still wish . . .

I SURE WOULD Love to have oNE of *those!*

Pay attention to what's good in your life, and say every day . . .

I AM GRATEFUL FOR WHAT I HAVE.

Have you ever done something you wish you hadn't? You might get mad at yourself and think . . .

I can't believe I forgot my sweater. I always forget everything!

Keep positive and say to yourself . . .

I LEARN FROM MY MISTAKES AND MOVE ON.

When it comes to taking
care of the world you live
in, you could think . . .

Instead, think...

I CARE FOR MY HOME, THE EARTH.

If people around you
have nothing good to say,
it can bring you down . . .

"It's too crowded!"

"I'm hot!"

Maybe they are Right!

"I'm so dizzy!"

Don't let others' moods change yours. Say . . .

I CHOOSE TO BE POSITIVE!

You might think you are not creative and that other kids have better ideas than you . . .

I can't decorate my bike. This is going to look awful!

Don't give up! Say to yourself ...

I AM FILLED WITH CREATIVE IDEAS.

When you see kids who look
or act different from you,
you might say to yourself . . .

I hope I don't have
to Ride with them.

Try to look past the differences you see on the outside. Think . . .

I SEE THE BEST IN EVERYONE.

Tips for Doing Affirmations

You can make up your own affirmations for anything you want to change in your life. For example . . .

1. Always start an affirmation with positive words such as:
I can, I am, I do, I have.

2. Say your affirmation over and over, whenever you think of it.

3. Say an affirmation especially when you are having a lot of unhappy/negative thoughts.

4. Look in the mirror and say your positive affirmations out loud.

5. Write your affirmations down in a notebook or journal.

6. Make a sign with your positive affirmation and hang it where you can see it every day (like on your mirror or bulletin board).

7. Close your eyes and picture what you want—this is an affirmation.

We hope you enjoyed this Hay House book.
If you'd like to receive our online catalog featuring additional information on
Hay House books and products, or if you'd like to find out more about the
Hay Foundation, please contact:

Hay House, Inc.
P.O. Box 5100
Carlsbad, CA 92018-5100

(760) 431-7695 or (800) 654-5126
(760) 431-6948 (fax) or (800) 650-5115 (fax)
www.hayhouse.com® • www.hayfoundation.org

Published and distributed in Australia by: Hay House Australia Pty. Ltd., 18/36 Ralph St., Alexandria NSW 2015
Phone: 612-9669-4299 • Fax: 612-9669-4144 • www.hayhouse.com.au

Published and distributed in the United Kingdom by: Hay House UK, Ltd., Astley House, 33 Notting Hill Gate, London W11 3JQ
Phone: 44-20-3675-2450 • Fax: 44-20-3675-2451 • www.hayhouse.co.uk

Published and distributed in the Republic of South Africa by:
Hay House SA (Pty), Ltd., P.O. Box 990, Witkoppen 2068
Phone/Fax: 27-11-467-8904
www.hayhouse.co.za

Published in India by: Hay House Publishers India,
Muskaan Complex, Plot No. 3, B-2, Vasant Kunj,
New Delhi 110 070 • Phone: 91-11-4176-1620
Fax: 91-11-4176-1630 • www.hayhouse.co.in

Distributed in Canada by: Raincoast Books, 2440 Viking Way,
Richmond, B.C. V6V 1N2 • Phone: 1-800-663-5714
Fax: 1-800-565-3770 • www.raincoast.com

Take Your Soul on a Vacation

Visit **www.HealYourLife.com®** to regroup, recharge, and reconnect with
your own magnificence. Featuring blogs, mind-body-spirit news, and
life-changing wisdom from Louise Hay and friends.

Visit **www.HealYourLife.com** today!